SAPPHO · POEMS

SAPPHO · POEMS

A New Version

*Translated from the Ancient Greek
and with an Introduction by Willis Barnstone*

SUN &
MOON

CLASSICS

90

LOS ANGELES
SUN & MOON PRESS
1998

Sun & Moon Press
A Program of The Contemporary Arts Educational Project, Inc.
a nonprofit corporation
6026 Wilshire Boulevard, Los Angeles, California 90036
website: http://www.sunmoon.com

First Sun & Moon Press edition 1998
10 9 8 7 6 5 4 3 2 1

This book was made possible, in part, through contributions to
The Contemporary Arts Educational Project, Inc., a nonprofit corporation.

Cover: Gino De Dominicus, *No*, 1981–82
Museum of Modern Art, New York
Mr. and Mrs. Sid R. Bass Fund
Reprinted by permission.
Design: Katie Messborn
Typography: Guy Bennett

LIBRARY OF CONGRESS CATALOGING IN PUBLICATION DATA
Sappho
Poems
Translated from the Ancient Greek
with an Introduction by Willis Barnstone
p. cm (Sun & Moon Classics: 90)
ISBN: 1-55713-358-1
1. Title. 11. Author 111. Translator
811'.54

Printed in the United States of America on acid-free paper.

Contents

One day in the late autumn of 1959, I spent an unexpected evening with Sappho. We were at the house of William McCulloh, professor of classics at Wesleyan University, and after a drink Bill introduced me to Sappho who was lying in *Lyra Graeca* (a Loeb Classical Library bilingual volume edited by J.M. Edmonds in 1928), looking disturbed and trapped. It was enough that time, popes, and anciently buried Egyptian trash dumps had largely reduced her some five hundred poems to fragments and gossip. Now a Cambridge don, Mr. Edmonds, had come to her rescue and filled in the lost lines with his own conjectured Greek verse. His inventions, often half or whole lines, were bracketed. He bequeathed us a co-authored Greek text by Sappho and Edmonds. For the Loeb edition he also translated his expanded Greek text into "literal" prose English, which subsequently became the basis for contemporary translations of Sappho in English. The wondrous versions by Mary Barnard, which for the first time gave us superb poems by Sappho in English and to whom every modern translator is in literary debt, are based on Professor Edmonds' English translations of his Greek conjectures. In emending the Greek to his own dreams, Edmonds chose a thankless way of making incoherent Sapphic fragments intelligible.

After meeting Sappho, I decided on the spot to know her better and chose a way.

In addition to the Edmonds' temptation, there are other ways of facing Sappho's badly mutilated originals. Recent good literary translations have both rejected Edmonds' divinations in toto and left the unintelligible spots as they were, undeciphered and emphasized by marking missing words and passages with multiple dots and blank spaces. A third way is to make reasonable guesses at syntactic connections between isolated letters, words, and phrases in order to let Sappho sing intelligibly in English. Where the Greek source leaves no extended sense, one should forget it or make a close version for an appendix.

As a poet and a student of Greek, I have chosen the third way, which is to contend with the gaps. I've made reasonable guesses, based on the Greek texts and contexts, for turning sometimes disparate words and phrases into ordinary speech. After some study the English version suddenly is apparent, its meaning inevitable and surprisingly obvious. This search and study I feel is my duty, an obligation to Sappho if one wants to see her read in English. Although in *The Poetics of Translation,* I don't deal with the specific problem of fragmentary texts I suggest here, as a principle, that if a very fragmentary work is to be rendered into English it must function not only as a gloss for reading the original but come through with the dignity and excitement of an original text. Anything less is to traduce Sappho.

Having so pontificated, I should add that my tenets should be warily scrutinized in the light of largely contrary convictions as displayed by, among others, Guy Davenport and Jim Powell in their skilled and masterful versions.

There is an old extremist, literalist argument against *any* multivalent, aesthetic treatment of a literary text, but that is a long sad story—and the one most frequently inspected in essays on translation. Once, however, one is committed to the goal of remaining faithful to the aesthetic quality of the original, to making a poem a poem, then Sappho becomes one of the most pleasant persons in the world to read. She appears in her naked Greek and to read her abroad she requires an attractive outfit in English. I sought every clue in Greek and English to have the version move from broken lines to a fresh, natural, and original poem. One goes back and forth between languages in the search. Ultimately, the last ordering is in English, coming at that instant when it flashes together. In all the translations I have done over the past decades, nothing has offered the magic and pleasure of Sappho as she suddenly acquires form and feeling in her English version.

When William McCulloh and I began to conspire about the Greek lyric poets, we planned a book in which I would translate the poems, he compose the headnotes and metrical index, and we collaborate on introductions. Three years later, in 1962, *Greek Lyric Poetry* appeared in which the canon of Sappho was included. Thereafter I worked alone on a bilingual edition of only Sappho, with scholarly apparatus, and that appeared in 1965 as *Sappho: Lyrics in the Original Greek with Translations.* Over the years I tinkered with the Sappho as it appeared in diverse editions of the *Greek Lyric Poetry.*

When I left Sappho—and at the time I knew her lines by heart—I strayed into koine Greek of the Septuagint and Gospels. Then here in California, thirty-five years after the first evening with her, I was happily visited by a similar *coup de foudre.* It was time. Hence this revised version, with a dozen newly deciphered poems. I experienced the same thrill of working with a fragment, now with slightly different fingers, until suddenly came the click.

To read Sappho is a privilege as it is to read her companion poets, the Sumerian Enheduanna, the Jewish woman speaker in the Song of Songs, and the Japanese diarist Izumi Shikibu. During a lifetime, Sappho has, along with the poems of Constantine Cavafy, San Juan de la Cruz, and Antonio Machado, sustained me. What a joy it has been to reread and revise her. I hope the reader will share some of these reckless pleasures.

—WILLIS BARNSTONE
Oakland, November, 1994

Supreme Sight on the Black Earth

Supreme Sight on the Black Earth

Some say cavalry and others claim
infantry or a fleet of long oars
is the supreme sight on the black earth.
I say it is

the one you love. And easily proved.
Didn't Helen, who far surpassed all
mortals in beauty, desert the best
of men, her king,

and sail off to Troy and forget
her daughter and her dear parents? Merely
Aprhodite's gaze made her readily bend
and led her far

from her path. These tales remind me now
of Anaktoria who isn't here,
yet I
for one

would rather see her warm supple step
and the sparkle of her face than watch all
the chariots in Lydia and footsoldiers armored
in glittering bronze.

16

Alone

The moon and the Pleiades
are set. It is midnight
and time spins away.
I lie in my bed alone.

168B

Seizure

To me he seems like a god
the man who sits facing you
and hears you near as you speak
softly and laugh

in a sweet echo that jolts
the heart in my ribs. For now
as I look at you my voice
is empty and

can say nothing as my tongue
cracks and slender fire is quick
under my skin. My eyes are dead
to light, my ears

pound, and sweat pours over me.
I convulse, greener than grass,
and feel my mind slip as I
go close to death,

yet I must suffer all things,
being poor.

31

Homecoming

You came
when I was longing for you,
and to my heart suffering in passion's fire
you were
delicious ice.

48

Blast of Love

Like a mountain whirlwind
punishing the oak trees,
love shattered my heart.

47

About Kleis

But if
you looked
at me
the gods
gave me
riches.

The wicked,
then my prayer
in darkness.
Is it much?
Do I care?
You grip me
while I live.

    (Voight) 213A,g

Recalling a Letter Atthis Wrote Me

"Sappho, if you don't come out of your room,
I swear I'll stop loving you.

O rise and free your lovely strength
from the bed and shine on us.
Take off your Chian nightgown,

and like a pure lily by a spring
bathe in the water. Our Kleis
will bring a saffron blouse and violet

tunic from your chest. We will place
a clean mantle on you, and crown
your hair with flowers. So come, darling,

with your beauty that maddens us,
and you, Praxinoa, roast the nuts
for our breakfast. One of the gods

is good to us, for on this day, you,
Sappho, most beautiful of women,
will come with us to your white city

of Mytilene, like a mother
among her daughters." Dearest Atthis,
after all these words to us, to me,

can you now forget all these days?

92

Friend, You Are Gone, But Remember Me

Honestly, I wish I were dead!
Although you too cried bitterly

when you left and said to me,
"Ah, what a nightmare it is now.
Sappho, I swear I go unwillingly."

And I answered, "Go, and be happy.
But remember me, for surely you
know how we worshiped you. If not,

then I want to remind you of all
the exquisite days
we two shared; how

you took garlands of violets,
crocuses and roses, and when by my side
you tied them round you in soft bands,

and you took many flowers
and flung them in loops
about your sapling throat,

how the air was rich in a scent
of queenly spices made of myrrh
you rubbed smoothly on your limbs,

and on soft beds, gently, your desire
for delicate young women
was satisfied,

and how there was no dance and no
holy shrine
we two didn't share,

no sound,
no
grove."

94

From Her Exile

For you, Kleis, I have no
embroidered headband and no idea
where to find one while Myrsilos

rules Mytilene. A bright
ribbon reminds me of those days
when we were not wasting away

and our enemies were in exile.

    98b

To Atthis

I loved you, Atthis, long ago
when you were like a small child with no charm.

49

To Eros

You burn me.

96

The Moon

Stars surrounding the marvelous moon
hide their sparkling forms
when in her full roundness she glows
over the whole earth.

34

Vision

Go so that
we can see
Lady Dawn
with gold arms,
which is
our fate.

6

Her Friend Far Off in Sardis

You are far in Sardis now
but you think of us constantly

and of the life we shared. I saw
you as a goddess and your dancing
left me profoundly happy.

Now you shine among Lydian women
like the rosy-fingered moon
rising after sundown, erasing all stars

nearest you and pouring light equally
across the salt sea
and over densely flowered meadows

lucent under dew. Your light spreads
on roses and tender thyme
and blooming honey lotus.

Often while you wander you remem-
ber me, gentle Atthis,
and desire eats away at your heart

for me to come.

To Kydro

I'm waiting
to see you, offer
gifts for a
safe arrival.
Much labor
in voyage,
and to you
I say, I
am coming.

19

To Aphrodite

On your dappled throne, eternal
Aphrodite, cunning daughter of Zeus,
I beg you, don't crush my heart
with love's pain

but come to me now, if ever before
you heard my remote cry, and yielded,
slipping from your father's house
of gold and came,

yoking birds to your chariot.
Beautiful sparrows took you suddenly
on whirring, fast-beating wings from
heaven through mid sky

down to the dark earth. O blessed
one, a smile on your deathless face,
you asked me what was wrong,
why did I call you,

what did my mad heart want to
happen. "This time whom shall I
persuade to love you? Who
is shunning you, Sappho?

Let her run away, soon she'll pursue
you; scorn your gifts, soon she'll bribe
you. Not love you? She will love you,
even unwillingly."

So come to me once again and free me
from blunt agony. Labor
and fill my heart with fire. Stand near,
and be my ally.

I

The Herald

Nightingale, with your lovely
   voice,
you are
the herald of spring.

   136

Aphrodite of the Flowers at Knossos
Coming Down from Heaven's Mountain

Leave Crete and come to this holy temple
where your graceful grove of apple trees
circles an altar smoking with frank-
    incense.

Here ice water babbles through the apple branches
and roses leave shadow on the ground
and bright shaking leaves pour down pro-
    found sleep.

In our meadow where the horses graze
amid wild blossoms of the spring and
anise shoots fill soft winds with a-
    roma

of honey, love goddess, pour heaven's
nectar carefully into gold wineglasses
and mingle our celebration with sud-
    den joy.

Myth

All would
agree
my tongue
tells mythical
tales
of a greater
man.

18

Weathercock

Brightness in Time of Storm

Brightness. With luck we'll reach
the harbor, solid ground
for our black ships.

We are sailors under great gales,
hoping for dry land
to sail to alive with our cargo.

The sky is transforming.
Awash in the storm we have many
urgent labors ahead. Dry land.

20

To Her Brother Charáxos

By now I'm sick

of your giving away cheap
your fine and noble
being to your friends. I'm swollen

with reproach.
Have your fill of them.
I understand,

but there are
other minds
and other gods in the world.

3

A Prayer to Aphrodite and the Sea Nymphs to Protect Her Brother Charáxos

Cypris and sea nymphs, I beg you
to sail my brother home safely
and let him accomplish the world's
things in his heart

as he atones for former errors
and carries joy to his friends
and disaster to enemies. We've
worried enough.

Let him honor me, his sister.
I would be free of black torment.
In early days he suffered cruelly,
citizens accused.

Was it over millet seed?
Pure Cyprian, will you put aside
your anger and liberate him from
more sorrows?

5

Dorícha

Arrogantly
Dorícha commands
him, yes, to come
or to stay,
the luck of
a young man.

6

About My Brother's Lover

Cyprian, let her feel your needles.
Don't let Dorícha crow about getting him
to come back on his knees, lusting for your
body a second time.

15

your face
r Hermione
compares with you. I'm overcome as if by
blond Helen's beauty

among mortal women. Listen. If you
were near, you'd free me from all worries
and on dewy banks (even of Acheron)
I'd stay awake all night.

24

Return, Gongyla

Your lovely face.
When absent,
the pain of unpleasant
winter.

O Gongyla, my darling rose,
put on your milk-white gown. I want
you to come back quickly. For my
desire feeds on

your beauty. Each time I see your gown
I am made weak and happy. I too
blamed the Cyprus-born. Now I pray
she will not seek

revenge, and may she soon allow
you, Gongyla, to come to me
again: you whom of all women
I most desire.

23

Her Friends

No, my heart
can never
change toward
you who are so
beautiful.

41

Impossible Yet

Impossible for it
to happen, for her
to come,
yet I pray for the surprise
of sharing, among all
people, her.

16

Let Sleeping Dogs Lie

Don't stir up
small heaps
of beach refuse.

143

To My Girlfriends

Dear companions, today
I will sing beautifully
and you will be happy.

160

Quickly Right Now

You were once a tender child.
Now come and sing. Talk and grant me
your beauty. Be generous
with your gracefulness.

We are walking to a wedding.
You know all that, but send your young
women away as quickly as you can.
Let the gods

keep their way. We mortals have no
road to high Olympos.

27

To Lady Hera

Be near me, Lady Hera, while I pray
for your graceful form to appear as once
it came to the Atreídai when they asked
for you, those dazzling kings

who accomplished many labors, first
around the city of Troy, then on the ocean,
sailing for this island, Lesbos. They couldn't
finish their voyage

till calling on you, Zeus, helper of wanderers,
and Dionysos, Thyrone's lovely child.
So be kind as in the ancient days
and help me now,

holy and beautiful goddess,
so we women

can sail safely
to the shrine.

17

Betrayal and Song

You have done wrong, Mika,
and I will not concur.
You have chosen women friends
from the villainous house of Pittakos,
yet now I hear a honey voice
singing
from the clear-voiced nightingale
in the dewy branches.

D70/LP71

Weathercocks

I am conscious
how often
those whom I treated
most kindly
especially injure me now.

26

Gone

You have forgotten me
or you love someone else more than me.

129

Annoyance

Never before, O Irana, have I found you
more repulsive than today.

91

Eros

Bittersweet, irrepressible love
loosens my limbs and I tremble,

yet, Atthis, the mere thought of me repels you
and you fly off to Andromeda.

130,131

Her Rival's Pedigree

I wish Andromeda, daughter of the house
of Polyanax, a bright good morning.

155

For a Rival

Sappho, why do you condemn the rich joys
    of Aphrodite?

    133b

Rival

I have lost, and you, Andromeda,
have made an excellent exchange.

133a

Andromeda, What Now?

Can this farm girl all spiffed up
in country finery compel your heart
when she hasn't got the brains
to wear her rags above her ankles?

57

Trial

When anger floods my chest
I bite my tongue, not to bark.

158

Virginity, Virginity

Dancers

The moon appeared in all her fullness
as virgins took their place around an altar.

In old days Cretan women danced
in perfect rhythm around a love altar,
crushing the soft flowering grass.

   154, Incert. 16

Wedding of Andromache

Cyprus. The herald came. The swift-running messenger came,
telling of the wedding's undying glory in all of Asia,

"Hektor and his companions bring sparkling-eyed, delicate
    Andromache
from holy Thebes and Plakía's flowing waters,
taking her on their ships over the salt sea,
with her many gold bracelets, fragrant purple robes,
    exquisite adornments,
and countless silver drinking jars and ivory."

So the herald spoke. And Hektor's dear father sprang to his feet
and the word spread from friend to friend throughout
    the spacious city.

Instantly, the sons of Ilios, founder of Troy,
harnessed the mules to carriages with smooth-running wheels,
and a big crowd of women and tender-ankled girls
    climbed on board.

Priam's daughters came in their own cars
and all the young unmarried men led out their stallions
and yoked them to greatly spirited chariots.

They moved like gods
                holy
        and all set out for Troy
            in a confusion of sweet-voiced flutes, citharas,
    and small crashing cymbals
and young girls sang a loud heavenly song
whose wonderful echo touched the ether of the sky.
Everywhere in the streets
were bowls and chalices.
Myrrh and cassia and incense rode on the wind.
Old women sang happily
and all the men sang out with thrilling force,
calling on Paian Apollo, the Master Archer skilled
    in the lyre. They all
sang to godlike Hektor and Andromache.

44

Paralysis

Mother darling, I can't work the loom,
for sleek Aphrodite has almost crushed
and broken me with desire for a boy.

102

Pathos

I long and hunger,
my pain drips.

36, 37

World

I couldn't hope
to touch the sky
with my two arms.

52

Pleasure

I will lay down
the limbs of my body on soft
cushions.

46

Sleep

May you sleep on your soft girlfriend's breasts.

126

Dialogue

Cyprus-born, in dream we two were talking.

134

Voice of a Poem

Come, holy tortoise shell, my lyre,
speak to me and find your voice.

118

Your Luminous Art

No woman I think will ever outshine
your skill—no woman who will ever
look into sunlight.

58

Was It the Muses?

Someone honored me, giving me
the secret of their craft.

32

Exhortation to Learning

A handsome man guards his image a while;
a good man will one day take on beauty.

50

Wealth and Virtue

Wealth without virtue is no harmless neighbor.
Blend them and walk the peak of happiness.

148

Affirmations

You ask for little,
you are carried away by what is sweet
and know about it
and comes the forgetting.

Someone might say no
but I shall love
as long as there is breath in me.
That's my way.

I say I've been a steady friend.
I've had grief and bitterness
yet know this (and it's better)
I shall love.

88

Pigeons Playing Dead

The hearts in the pigeons grow cold
and the wings drop to their sides.

42

Eros

Eros descended from heaven dressed in a purple cape.

54

Don't Go Bareheaded, Dika

Dika, take some shoots of dill and loop them
with your tender hands about your lovely hair.
The blessed Graces love her who wears flowers
but turn their backs on one who goes plain.

81

On Fabrics from the Island of Amorgos

She wore around her the soft fine linen robes from
  Amorgos

    100

Hair Yellower Than Torchlight

My mother always said
that in her youth she was
exceedingly in fashion

wearing a purple ribbon
looped in her hair. But the girl
whose hair is yellower

than torchlight need wear no
colorful ribbons from Sardis
or some Ionian city. A

garland of fresh flowers will do.

98a

A Ring

Silly woman. Why do you lose your head
crooning about a ring?

    Incert. 5a

Love Token

By the way, Aphrodite,

here is a perfumed kerchief
of porphyry color, a rare gift sent
from far Phokaia.

101

Evening Star

Hesperos of all stars is the most beautiful.

104b

Evening Star

Hesperos, you bring home all the bright dawn
    scattered,
bring home the sheep,
bring home the goat, bring the child home to
    its mother.

104a

Artemis's Virginity*

Artemis swore a severe oath to gold-haired Phoibos,
whom Koios's daughter bore after she lay with Zeus,
the famous lord of high clouds. She swore by
    his beard:

"I will remain a virgin hunting upon the peaks
of solitary mountains. Grant me this favor."
So she spoke and the father of the blessed gods
    consented.

Now gods and mortals call her Virgin Hunter
and Slayer of Deer,
and Eros, loosener of cords holding in reluctant
    thighs,

never comes near her.

44a

* *Attributed to Alkáios by Lobel and Page, to Sappho by Max Treu, and included
among the Sappho texts by David Campbell.*

The Virgin

Like a sweet apple reddening on the high
tip of the topmost branch and forgotten
by the apple pickers, not missed but beyond their
   reach.

Like a hyacinth crushed in the mountains
by men shepherding; lying trampled on the earth
yet blooming purple.

   105a,c

Shall I?

I don't know what to do.
I say yes—and then no.

51

Wonder

Do I still long for my virginity?

107

Outside the Window

We virgins will spend all night long
near the door, singing of the love
between you and your bride. Her robed
limbs are violets.

Wake and call out young bachelors
of your age and walk the streets,
and we'll see less sleep tonight than
the bright-voiced nightingale.

30

End of a Party

Night
has tossed peace into confusion.
The mind
collapses.
Yet come, my friends,
for soon it will be day.

43

The Guard Outside the Bridal Chamber

The doorkeeper's feet are seven fathoms long,
and ten shoemakers used up five coarse ox hides
in cobbling together his giant sandals.

110

The Bride and Virginity Talk

"Virginity, virginity, where have you gone, deserting
    me?"
"Never again will I come to you. Never again will
    I come."

114

Song for the Bride

Keep in mind, O groom, there never was
 a woman like her.

113

Taking Care of the Groom

Carpenters, raise the roofbeams
and we'll sing out *Hymen*.
Get the carpenters to raise the roof
and we'll sing out *Hymen*.
The groom is on his way. He is like
the wargod Ares, yet even more
towering than a tall mortal.

III

Hermes and Wine

There a bowl of ambrosia
was mixed
and Hermes took the pitcher and poured wine for the gods.
They all held out their glasses,
made libations, and prayed for marvelous things
for the groom.

141

To the Groom

Who are you, lovely groom?
You are a slender sapling.

116

Etched by Love

Innocence

I don't have a rancorous spirit
but the simple heart of a child.

120

My Daughter Kleis

I have a beautiful daughter who is
like a gold flower. I wouldn't trade
my darling Kleis for all Lydia or even
the whole lovely island of Lesbos.

132

A Girl

One day I watched a tender girl
picking some wild flowers.

122

Behind a Laurel Tree

You lay in wait
behind a laurel tree,

and everything
was pleasant:

you a woman
wanderer like me.

I barely heard you,
my darling;

you came in your
trim garments,

and suddenly: beauty
of your garments.

   62a

Heart

Don't try to bend a crazed heart.

Incert. 5b

Then

In gold sandals
dawn like a thief
fell upon me.

123

Where Are We?

Soft girl,
once more I
have wandered

    Incert. 5c

A Rival

By now they've had their fill of Gorgo.

144

Return

I have flown to you like a child to her mother.

Incert. 25

Writing a Poem

Muses, leave your gold house
and again come to me now.

127

To an Ignorant Woman Who Lacks the Flowers Invented by the Muses

When you lie dead no one will remember
or miss you, for you have no share in the roses
of Piería. Unseen here and in the house of Hades,
you'll flitter invisible among dark corpses.

    Incert. 55

Talking with the Poet Alkáios

Alkáios says:
Violet-haired, holy, honey-smiling Sappho,
I wish to speak to you but shame disarms me.
. . .
Sappho replies:
If you cared at all for what's right and good
and your tongue weren't dreaming up nastiness,
shame would not be hiding in your eyes
and you would speak out your real desires.

Alkáios 84, Sappho 137

To a Handsome Man

If you are my friend, stand up before me
and scatter the grace that's in your eyes.

138

The Death of Adonis

Our tender Adonis is dying, Aphrodite.
What can we do?
Beat your breasts, women, and tear your dresses.

140

The Beauty of Her Women

Mnasidíka has a lovelier body
than even our soft Gyrinno's.

882

Cicada

Rubbing its wings incessantly,
a cicada pours flaming summer
over the earth
in luminous song.

    Voight 101a

Sleep

The black sleep of night closes my eyes.

151

Having Refused to Accept the Bitter with the Sweet

I don't want honey or the honey bee.

146

The Swan's Egg Bearing Castor and Pollux

They say that long ago Leda found an egg
coated entirely with the color of hyacinth.

166

Notice

The gods come
straightaway
to the tearless.

139

Rules of Love

Even if you lust for me, take
a younger woman to your bed.
I can't bear to share my body
where I hang on as the elder.

121

Time of Youth

How one day you will remember
that we too did things
in our youth,

many and beautiful things,
and in the city
we feel them sharply,

live near the boldness
of a man and hear
a fine small voice.

24a

Age and Light

Here is success for your tongue, my children,
the poems of the pear-breasted Muses,

which are the fine gifts for the singer
on the clear tortoise lyre,

yet old age already wrinkles my skin,
my black hair has faded to white,

my legs can no longer carry me,
once nimble like a dancing fawn's,

but what can I do?
To be ageless is impossible,

no more than can the pink-armed Dawn
not end in darkness on the earth

or keep her love for old Tithonos
who must waste away.

Yet I love refinement, and beauty and light
are for me the same as desire for the sun.

58

ream

dream on your black wings
u come when I am sleeping.

eet is the god but still I am
in agony and far from my strength,

for I had hope (none now) to share
something of the blessed gods,

nor was I so foolish
as to scorn pleasant toys.

Now may I have
all these things.

D67

An Epiphany About Gongyla, Hermes and Hades

Gongyla, is there no sign of you? No epiphany
of your presence? Hermes came
in a dream. O Lord,

I swear by my ally Aphrodite, I have no pleasure
in being on the earth. I care
only to die,

to watch the banks of Acheron plaited
with lotus, the dewy banks
of the river of Hades.

95

Sappho Angry with Her Daughter When She Sappho Was Dying

It would be wrong for us. It is not right
for mourning to enter a home of poetry.

150

Old Age

Of course I am downcast and tremble
with pity for my state
when old age and wrinkles cover me,

when Eros flies about
and I pursue the glorious young.
Pick up your lyre

and sing to us of her who wears
violets on her breasts. Sing especially
of her who is wandering.

21

No Oblivion

Someone, I tell you,
will remember us.

147

Sappho, I Loved You

Andromeda
forgot,

and I too
blamed you,

yet Sappho
I loved you.

In Cyprus I'm Queen
Aphrodite, a power

to you as sun of fire
is a glory to all.

Even in Hades
I am with you.

D68

Eros

Now in my
heart I
see clearly

a beautiful
face
shining,

etched
by love.

4

NOTE ON GREEK TEXTS

The Greek text used for these translations is, unless otherwise noted, from Edgar Lobel and Denys Page, *Poetarum Lesbiorum Fragmenta*, Oxford: Clarendon Press, 1955. I have also consulted Ernest Diel, *Anthologia Lyrica Graeca*, vol. 1, Leipzig, 1935; Max Treu, *Sappho*. Munich: E. Heimeran, 1954; and David A. Campbell, *The Loeb Classical Library*, vol. 1, *Sappho and Alcaeus*. Cambridge: Harvard University Press, 1982. Poem titles, in most cases, were derived from source context.

The glossary is an updated version that appeared in Willis Barnstone, *Sappho: Lyrics in the Original Greek with Translations*, New York: Doubleday Anchor, 1965.

GLOSSARY

Acheron. The river of Death running through Hades. It began in Thesprotia, Epiros, and disappeared underground in places where it was supposed to lead to Hades.

Achilles. Son of Peleus and the sea nymph (the Nereid) Thetis. He is the tragic hero of Homer's *Iliad*.

Adonis. Aphrodite's beautiful young lover. He was killed by a wild boar or by Ares or Hephaistos but was allowed to spend six months of each year upon the earth with Aphrodite, the remainder with Persephone in the underworld. Thus he was identified with the seeding and harvesting of crops and was worshiped, especially by women, as divinity of vegetation and fertility. In Sappho Adonis spends four months with Aphrodite, four months with Persephone, and four months alone.

Alkaios (Alcaeus). Born about 620 BC in Mytilene, Lesbos. A poet, contemporary and possible friend or lover of Sappho, he wrote lyric poems that deal with politics, love, drinking, the sea, in the Aiolic (Lesbian) dialect. The Alcaic strophe was imitated by Horace.

Amorgine. Of Amorgos, an island of the Aigaion Sea, one of the Sporades, known for its Amorgine linen. It was the birthplace of Semonides.

Anaktoria. One of Sappho's friends. One theory is that she left Sappho in order to marry and follow her husband to Sardis, where he was probably a soldier.

Andromache. The wife of Hector, the Trojan hero.

Andromeda. A rival of Sappho; perhaps a poet.

Aphrodite. Goddess of love, beauty, sea, flowers, and fertility. She was born in the seafoam (*aphros*) off the shore of Paphos in Kypros (Cyprus) and so is called variously Kypris (Cypris), Kyprian (Cyprian), Kypros-born (Cyprus-born), and the Paphian (of Paphos). As a symbol of passion and romantic love, she is a particular ally to Sappho and is mentioned by Sappho in the existing fragments more often than any other deity or person. The one complete poem attributed to Sappho is addressed to Aphrodite.

Apollo. Apollo and his twin sister Artemis were born in

Delos, children of Zeus and Leto. God of prophecy, music, medicine; as sun-god identified with Helios. He was the ideal of young, manly beauty and of civilized Greek man.

Ares. Greek war-god and personification of warrior type. In Rome he was the more popular Mars.

Artemis. Twin sister of Apollo (q.v.), she was the virgin goddess of the forest and hunting and of the moon.

Atreidai. Sons or descendants of Atreus, usually referring to Agamemnon and Menelaos.

Atthis. One of Sappho's friends, treated with deep affection in many peoms. Like Anaktoria (q.v.), she leaves Sappho.

Chian. Of the island of Chios, a large island south of Lesbos, near Asia Minor.

Cretan, Crete. Large island in the Aigaion with capital of Minoan civilization at Knossos.

Dika. Probably short for Mnasidika (q.v.), one of Sappho's friends.

Dionysos. God of vegetation, wine, and spiritual ecstasy, he was worshiped with orgiastic rites and often represents the counterpart of Apollonian moderation. Also called Bakchos (Bacchus).

Eros. God of love, child or attendant of Aphrodite. Sappho makes Eros the son of Gaia (Earth) and Ouranos (Sky) but she most often uses Eros to mean simply love; these many references are not cited here.

Gello. A woman who died young and became a demon or

ghost that haunted children, kidnaped them, or caused
their deaths.

Gongyla. One of Sappho's intimate friends.

Gorgo. A rival of Sappho's; perhaps also a poet.

Graces (Charites). Daughters of Zeus, personifications of
grace and beauty. They are friends of the Muses with
whom they live on Olympos; their favored art is poetry.

Gyara. An island in the Aigaion, one of the Kyklades.

Gyrinno, Gyrinna. One of Sappho's companions.

Hades (Aides: the unseen). Son of Kronos, god of the un-
derworld, where he reigns with his wife, Persephone,
over the souls of the dead. Hades also means the realm
of Hades.

Helen. Daughter of Zeus and Leda, a goddess of extraordi-
nary beauty. As the wife of Menelaos she was seduced
and abducted by Paris to Troy and so became the overt
cause of the Trojan War.

Hekate. An earth goddess associated with sorcery, magic,
ghosts, and worshiped at night at crossroads.

Hektor. Son of Priam, husband of Andromache and hero of
the defense of Troy. He was killed by Achilles in Homer's
Iliad.

Hephaistos. Lame god of fire and the crafts. Despite Ares'
claim, Hephaistos fashioned a net in which he caught
Ares and Aphrodite in their love-making.

Hera. Sister and wife of Zeus, Hera was queen of the gods
and patron goddess of marriage.

Hermes. Athletic son of Zeus and Maia, he was the cupbearer and messenger of the gods, and guide of the dead to Hades. He was also god of commerce, travelers, good luck, and was credited with the invention of music, the lyre, numbers, the alphabet, gymnastics, etc.

Hermione. Daughter of Menelaos and Helen. Her beauty did not match the beauty of her mother, Helen.

Hesperos. The evening star, son of Astraios or Kephalos or Atlas and Eos (Dawn), and father of the Hesperides.

Hymen, Hymenaios. God of marriage, a handsome youth whom it was customary to invoke at Greek weddings by singing Hymen, O Hymen, in the hymneal or bridal song.

Ida. The herald or messenger who is probably from Ida, a mountain area near Troy. In the *Iliad,* he appears as the chief herald of Troy.

Ilios (Ilus). Son of Tros and founder of Ilium (Troy). Ilium was the city of Ilios but was also called Troy after his father, Tros. Homer's *Iliad* deals with the siege of Ilium (Troy).

Ilium (Troy). City of Ilios (q.v.).

Ionian. Greeks in an area of the west coast of Asia Minor

Jason. Leader of the Argonauts who set sail in the Argo to find the Golden Fleece, which he hoped to bring his uncle Pelias in exchange for his patrimony. He obtained the fleece with the help of Medea, whom he later married.

Kalliope. Muse of heroic poetry (See Muses).

Kleis. Name of Sappho's daughter, also her mother, and perhaps a friend.

Knossos. Ancient capital of the Minoan kingdom and site of the palace of Minos, which has been associated with the labyrinth and the minotaur (the bull of Minos).

Koios. A Titan, mother of Leto and hence grandmother of Apollo and Artemis.

Kyprian (Cyprian) or *Kypris (Cypris).* One from Kypros (Cyprus), in this case Aphrodite.

Kypros (Cyprus), Kypros-born (Cyprus-born). The large Greek island of Kypros (Cyprus), near the coast of Syria, was one of the chief seats of worship of Aphrodite. The Kypros-born (Cyprus-born) is Aphrodite.

Kythereia. Of the island of Kythera, southeast of Lakonia, Peloponnesos, a seat of worship of Aphrodite. Hence the goddess was called Kythereia. There was also a tradition that Aphrodite rose from the sea near Kythera (See *Aphrodite*).

Leda. Mother of Helen, the Dioskouroi, and in some versions Klytemnestra, and wife of Tyndareus. She was seduced by Zeus, who came to her, as readers of Yeats know, in the form of a swan. Another version, to which Sappho alludes, has Nemesis lay an egg which Leda found and cared for and from which came Helen.

Meniskos. Father of Pelagon.

Mika. Probably a shortened form of Mnasidika (q.v.), a rival who had gone over to the rival house of Penthilos, ruling nobles of Mytilene.

Mnasidika. A friend of Sappho's who appears to have deserted her (See Mika).

Muses. Daughters of Zeus and Mnemosyne (Memory), the nine Muses lived on Mount Helikon, where they presided over the arts and sciences.

Myrsilos. Tyrant of Mytilene who probably caused the exile of Alkaios and Sappho.

Mytilene, Mitylene. Ancient and modern capital of Lesbos, where Sappho spent much of her life. The dialect of Lesbos was Aiolic, in which Sappho and Alkaios wrote.

Nereids. Sea Nymphs, fifty daughters of Nereus, the old man of the sea.

Nereus. Son of Pontos, husband of the Oceanid Doris, and father of the Nereids, Nereus was the wise old man of the sea.

Niobe. Daughter of Tantalos and wife of Amphion, Niobe boasted to Leto that her family was larger than Leto's, and to avenge this insult Leto's children, Apollo and Artemis, killed the twelve to twenty children of Niobe. Niobe became a stock figure of bereavement (see *Testimonia*).

Pandion. King of Athens whose daughters Philomela and Prokne were turned into a swallow and a nightingale. (Latin tradition reversed the order.) The presence of a swallow was often the sign of a forthcoming event.

Panormos. One of several Greek cities with this name where Aphrodite was worshiped, but not the most famous Panormos (Palermo) in Sicily. Palermo did not acquire its Greek name until after Sappho's time.

Paphian. Of Paphos, and therefore Aphrodite. Aphrodite

was born in the foam near the city of Paphos in Kypros (Cyprus)(see Aphrodite).

Paphos. (See Paphian and Aphrodite.)

Peitho. The personification of Persuasion, and the daughter or attendant of Aphrodite.

Pelagon. A fisherman.

Penthilos. A rival family of ruling nobles in Mytilene (see Mika, Mnasidika). Pittakos, Tyrant of Lesbos in Sappho's time, married the sister of Drakon, former ruler, who was the son of Penthilos.

Persephone. Closely associated with her mother, Demeter, Persephone was abducted by Hades and taken to the underworld. Her yearly return to earth signified the coming of spring.

Pierian. Of Pieria, a region of Thrace in Macedonia, where the Muses were first worshiped.

Phokaia. A city of Ionia in Asia Minor, southeast of Mytilene.

Plakia. A river near Thebes (q.v.) in the area near Troy.

Pleiades. Daughters of Atlas and virgin companions of Artemis. When pursued by the giant hunter Orion, their prayers were answered when they were changed into doves (*peleiades*) and placed among the stars.

Praxinoa. One of Sappho's companions.

Priam. King of Troy at time of the Achaian attack, father of Hektor.

Sappho. Born about 612 BC in Eresos or Mytilene, Lesbos, Sappho wrote lyric poems in her own Aiolic dialect in which she referred to herself as Psappho.

Sardis. Ancient city of Asia Minor and capital of the kingdom of Lydia.

Thebe, Thebes. Not the more famous cities of Boioteia or Egypt, but a holy city near Mount Ida in the Troad in which Andromache's father, Etion, was both king and high priest.

Thyone, Semele. A daughter of Kadmos and mother of Dionysos.

Timas. One of Sappho's companions.

Tithonos. Brother of Priam and lover of Eos (Dawn), who left him each morning. Through the prayers of Eos he became immortal but he did not retain his youth and so became synonymous with a decrepit old man.

Zeus. Son of Kronos and Rhea, brother of Poseidon, Hades, Hestia, Demeter, and Hera, who was also his wife, Zeus was father, by one means or another, of innumerable important divine progeny. He was the greatest of the Olympian gods, and, as the all-powerful director of thunder and lightning and giver of good and evil, his name was often interchangeable with supreme divinity.

SAPPHO

Sappho was born in about 612 BC in Eresos or Mytilene, small cities on the island of Lesbos. Being from Lesbos, she was geographically a Lesbian, and her love for her women companions became identified as "lesbian love." Sappho was married and had a daughter named Kleis. At one time, under the rule of Pittakos, she and her family were forced into internal political exile. Sappho was a prolific writer, writing seven or nine long books of poetry, but a thousand years of hostility under the early church destroyed most of her work. She is preserved in fragments, as citations in the works of classical authors, and on strips of papyrus found in Egypt (in the *Oxyrhynchuis Papyri*). Her single extant complete poem, "To Aphrodite," Longius quotes in his essay *On the Sublime*. While there are many ancient biographical references to her, these come from later periods and are unreliable. The best picture of her life and spirit emerges in the poems. Sappho was esteemed as the greatest lyric poet of Greek and Latin antiquity. Plato called her the tenth muse. In the first century the Latin poet Catullus dedicated his poems to his Lesbia (the poet from Lesbos). In Sappho we hear for the first time in the Western world the direct words of an individual woman. Skilled, complex, and powerful, she speaks with elemental and alarming grace. We hear the immediate sound of the lyric voice in love, in pathos, in solitude. It cannot be said that her candid song has ever been surpassed.

Willis Barnstone

Willis Barnstone lived for years in Greece. His own poems have appeared in *The Nation, The New Yorker, Partisan Review, The New Republic,* and *The Kenyon Review.* He is the author of *The Secret Reader: 501 Sonnets* and *The Poetics of Translation,* and has translated numerous books, including the poems of Saint John of the Cross, Antonio Machado, and Wang Wei (with Tony Barnstone). His *New and Selected Poems* was published in 1997, and his *Moonbook & Sunbook* was published in 1998. He also translated *The Cosmic Fragments of Heraclitus, Greek Lyric Poetry,* and a literary version of the New Testament.

SUN & MOON CLASSICS

MAC WELLMAN [USA]
The Land Beyond the Forest: Dracula AND *Swoop* 112
(1-55713-228-3, $12.95)
Two Plays: A Murder of Crows AND *The Hyacinth Macaw* 62
(1-55713-197-X, $11.95)

JOHN WIENERS [USA]
707 Scott Street 106 (1-55713-252-6, $12.95)

ÉMILE ZOLA [France]
The Belly of Paris 70 (1-55713-066-3, $14.95)

*

Individuals order from:
Sun & Moon Press
6026 Wilshire Boulevard
Los Angeles, California 90036
213-857-1115

Libraries and Bookstores in the United States and Canada
should order from:
Consortium Book Sales & Distribution
1045 Westgate Drive, Suite 90
Saint Paul, Minnesota 55114-1065
800-283-3572
FAX 612-221-0124

Libraries and Bookstores in the United Kingdom and on the Continent
should order from:
Password Books Ltd.
23 New Mount Street
Manchester M4 4DE, ENGLAND
0161 953 4009
INTERNATIONAL +44 61 953-4009
0161 953 4090